AUDIO
ACCESS
INCLUDED

THE POLICE

T0039921

Cover photo © Barry Schultz/RETNA

Tracking, mixing, and mastering by
Jake Johnson & Bill Maynard at Paradyme Productions
All guitars by Doug Boduch
Bass by Tom McGirr
Drums by Scott Schroedl
Keyboards by Warren Wiegratz
Additional keys by Jay Lechler

PLAYBACK+
Speed • Pitch • Balance • Loop

To access audio visit:
www.halleonard.com/mylibrary

1127-8836-7593-0216

ISBN 978-1-4234-4651-4

For all works contained herein:
Unauthorized copying, arranging, adapting, recording, Internet posting, public performance,
or other distribution of the music in this publication is an infringement of copyright.
Infringers are liable under the law.

Visit Hal Leonard Online at
www.halleonard.com

Contact us:
Hal Leonard
7777 West Bluemound Road
Milwaukee, WI 53213
Email: info@halleonard.com

In Europe, contact:
Hal Leonard Europe Limited
42 Wigmore Street
Marylebone, London, W1U 2RN
Email: info@halleonardeurope.com

In Australia, contact:
Hal Leonard Australia Pty. Ltd.
4 Lentara Court
Cheltenham, Victoria, 3192 Australia
Email: info@halleonard.com.au

GUITAR NOTATION LEGEND

THE MUSICAL STAFF shows pitches and rhythms and is divided by bar lines into measures. Pitches are named after the first seven letters of the alphabet.

TABLATURE graphically represents the guitar fingerboard. Each horizontal line represents a string, and each number represents a fret.

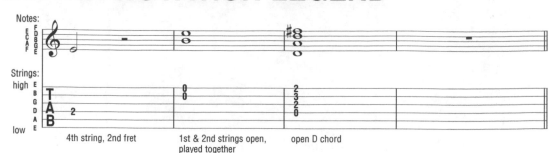

4th string, 2nd fret   1st & 2nd strings open, played together   open D chord

HALF-STEP BEND: Strike the note and bend up 1/2 step.

WHOLE-STEP BEND: Strike the note and bend up one step.

GRACE NOTE BEND: Strike the note and immediately bend up as indicated.

SLIGHT (MICROTONE) BEND: Strike the note and bend up 1/4 step.

BEND AND RELEASE: Strike the note and bend up as indicated, then release back to the original note. Only the first note is struck.

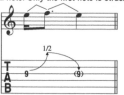

PRE-BEND: Bend the note as indicated, then strike it.

VIBRATO: The string is vibrated by rapidly bending and releasing the note with the fretting hand.

PALM MUTING: The note is partially muted by the pick hand lightly touching the string(s) just before the bridge.

HAMMER-ON: Strike the first (lower) note with one finger, then sound the higher note (on the same string) with another finger by fretting it without picking.

PULL-OFF: Place both fingers on the notes to be sounded. Strike the first note and without picking, pull the finger off to sound the second (lower) note.

LEGATO SLIDE: Strike the first note and then slide the same fret-hand finger up or down to the second note. The second note is not struck.

SHIFT SLIDE: Same as legato slide, except the second note is struck.

TRILL: Very rapidly alternate between the notes indicated by continuously hammering on and pulling off.

TAPPING: Hammer ("tap") the fret indicated with the pick-hand index or middle finger and pull off to the note fretted by the fret hand.

NATURAL HARMONIC: Strike the note while the fret-hand lightly touches the string directly over the fret indicated.

PINCH HARMONIC: The note is fretted normally and a harmonic is produced by adding the edge of the thumb or the tip of the index finger of the pick hand to the normal pick attack.

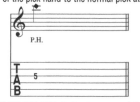

TREMOLO PICKING: The note is picked as rapidly and continuously as possible.

VIBRATO BAR DIVE AND RETURN: The pitch of the note or chord is dropped a specified number of steps (in rhythm), then returned to the original pitch.

VIBRATO BAR SCOOP: Depress the bar just before striking the note, then quickly release the bar.

VIBRATO BAR DIP: Strike the note and then immediately drop a specified number of steps, then release back to the original pitch.

Additional Musical Definitions

(accent) • Accentuate note (play it louder).

(staccato) • Play the note short.

D.S. al Coda • Go back to the sign (%), then play until the measure marked "***To Coda***," then skip to the section labelled "**Coda**."

D.C. al Fine • Go back to the beginning of the song and play until the measure marked "***Fine***" (end).

Fill • Label used to identify a brief melodic figure which is to be inserted into the arrangement.

N.C. • Harmony is implied.

• Repeat measures between signs.

• When a repeated section has different endings, play the first ending only the first time and the second ending only the second time.

CONTENTS

Page		Title
4		Can't Stand Losing You
10		De Do Do Do, De Da Da Da
16		Every Breath You Take
22		Message in a Bottle
27		Roxanne
32		Spirits in the Material World
36		Synchronicity II
43		Walking on the Moon

Can't Stand Losing You

Music and Lyrics by Sting

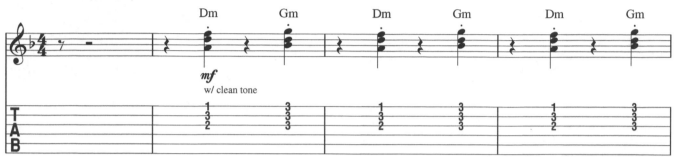

Intro
Moderately fast Rock ♩ = 144

mf
w/ clean tone

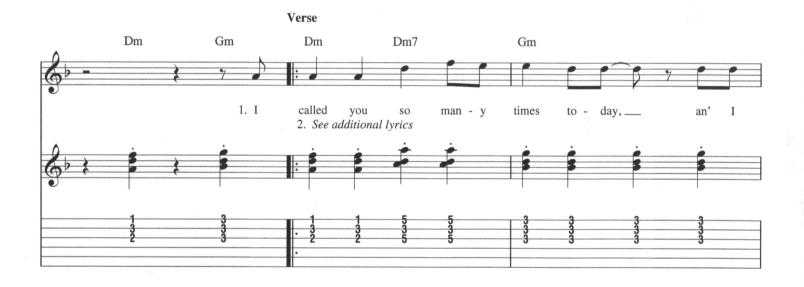

Verse

1. I called you so man-y times to-day, ___ an' I
2. *See additional lyrics*

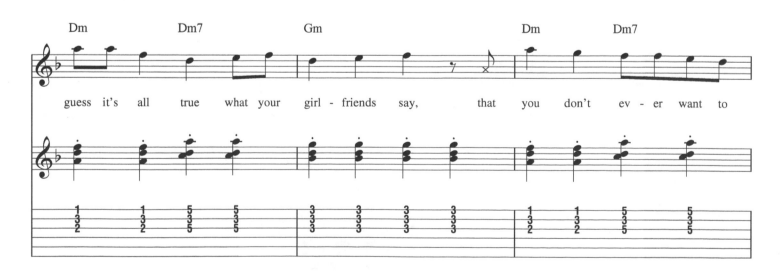

guess it's all true what your girl-friend say, that you don't ev-er want to

© 1978 G.M. SUMNER
Administered by EMI MUSIC PUBLISHING LIMITED
All Rights Reserved   International Copyright Secured   Used by Permission

see me a - gain, __ and your broth-er's gon - na kill me an' he's six feet ten. I

℆ Pre-Chorus

guess you'd call it cow - ard - ice, but I'm not pre - pared __ to go on __

2., 3. See additional lyrics.

w/ dist.

Chorus

__ like this. __ I __ can't, I can't, I can't stand los - in'. I __

P.M.

__ can't, I can't, I can't stand los - in'. I __ can't, I can't, I

P.M.

5

guess this is our last good- bye, ___ and you don't care so

I won't cry, and you'll be sor - ry when I'm dead, and

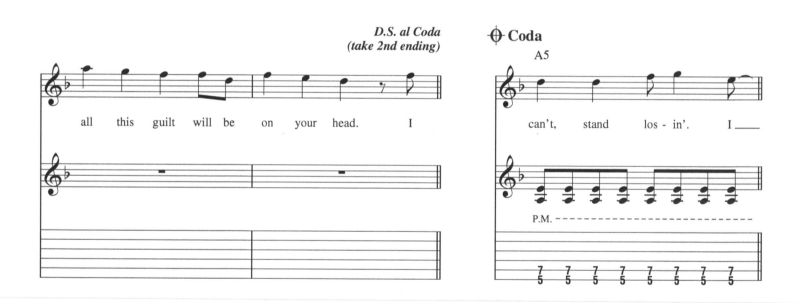

all this guilt will be on your head. I can't, stand los - in'. I ___

D.S. al Coda
(take 2nd ending)

✚ **Coda**

A5

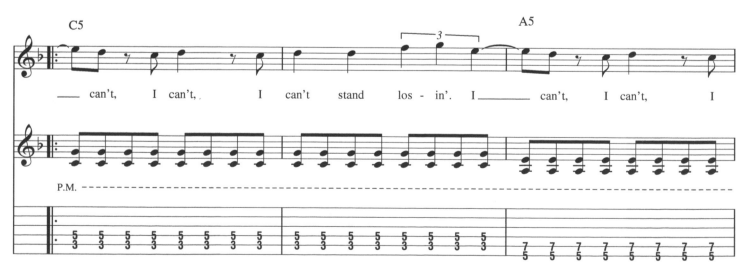

C5   A5

___ can't, I can't, I can't stand los - in'. I ___ can't, I can't, I

Additional Lyrics

2. I see you've sent my letters back,
   An' my L.P. records and they're all scratched.
   I can't see the point in another day
   When nobody listens to a word I say.

Pre-Chorus 2. You can call it lack of confidence,
   But to carry on livin' doesn't make no sense.

Pre-Chorus 3. I guess you'd call it suicide,
   But I'm too full to swallow my pride.

De Do Do Do, De Da Da Da

Music and Lyrics by Sting

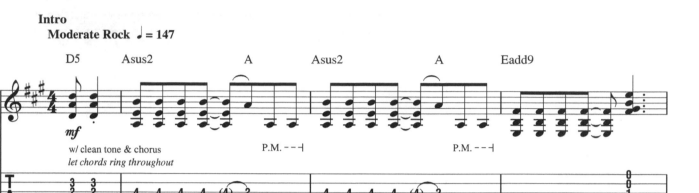

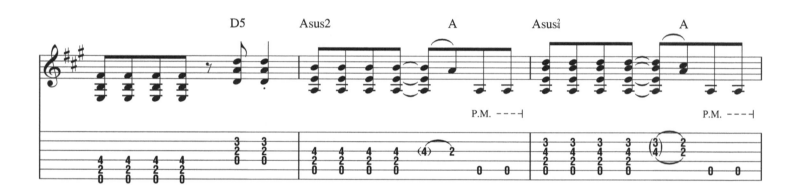

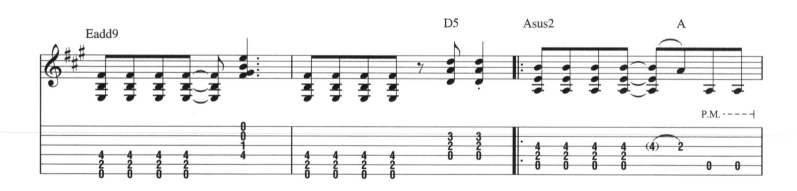

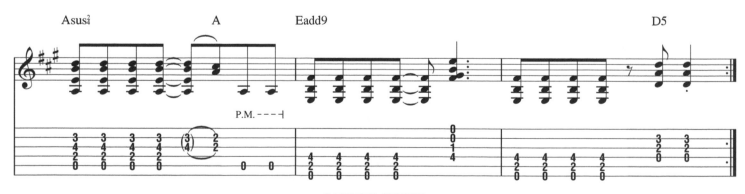

© 1980 G.M. SUMNER
Administered by EMI MUSIC PUBLISHING LIMITED
All Rights Reserved   International Copyright Secured   Used by Permission

from the banks __ of cha - os in __ my mind. __

Pre-Chorus

And when their el - o - quence __ es - capes __
See additional lyrics

__ me, __

their log - ic ties __

__ me up __ and rapes __ me.

do do do, de da da da, the mean-ing-less _ and all _

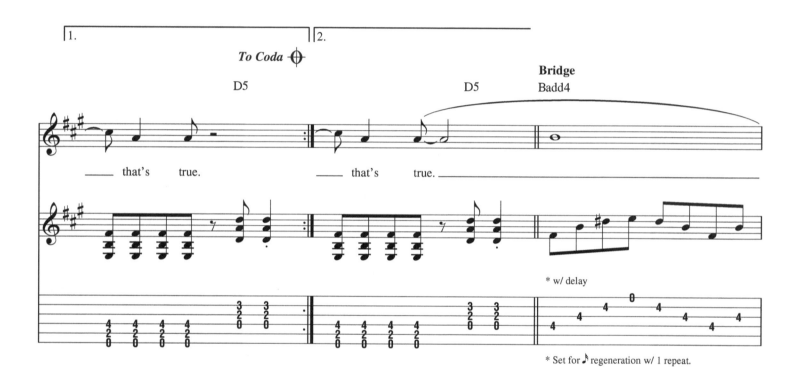

that's true.
that's true. _

Bridge

* w/ delay

* Set for ♪ regeneration w/ 1 repeat.

*Bass plays notes to right of slashes, next 5 meas.

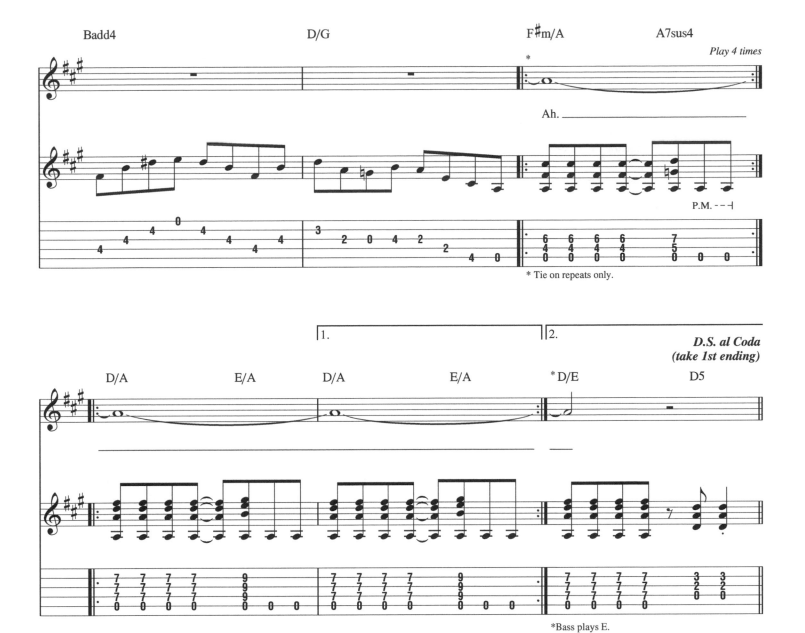

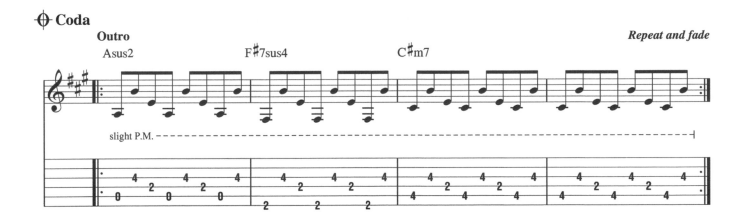

Additional Lyrics

2. Poets, priests and politicians have words to thank for their positions.
   Words that scream for your submission, and no one's jamming their transmission.

Pre-Chorus 2. 'Cause when their eloquence escapes you,
   Their logic ties you up and rapes you.

Every Breath You Take

Music and Lyrics by Sting

© 1983 G.M. SUMNER
Administered by EMI MUSIC PUBLISHING LIMITED
All Rights Reserved   International Copyright Secured   Used by Permission

18

Interlude

I keep cry - ing, ba - by, ba - by, please.

Oh, can't you

20

Message in a Bottle

Music and Lyrics by Sting

1. Just a cast - a - way, __ an is - land lost __ at sea, __
2.,3. *See additional lyrics*

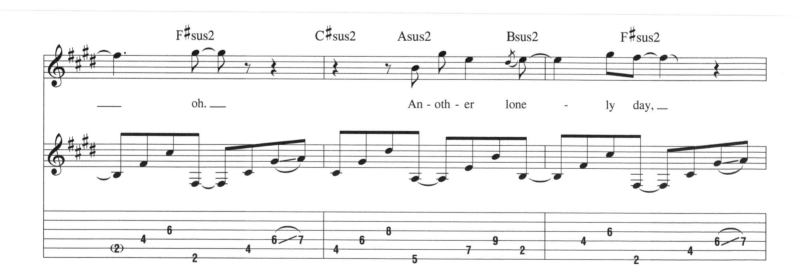

__ oh. __ An - oth - er lone - ly day, __

© 1979 G.M. SUMNER
Administered by EMI MUSIC PUBLISHING LIMITED
All Rights Reserved   International Copyright Secured   Used by Permission

Mes - sage in a bot - tle, yeah.

Oh. Mes - sage in a bot - tle, yeah.

D.S. al Coda

Additional Lyrics

2. A year has passed since I wrote my note.
   I should have known this right from the start.
   Only hope can keep me together.
   Love can mend your life, but love can break your heart.

3. Woke up this morning, I don't believe what I saw,
   Hundred billion bottles washed up on the shore.
   Seems I never noticed being alone.
   Hundred billion castaways, looking for a home.

Roxanne

Music and Lyrics by Sting

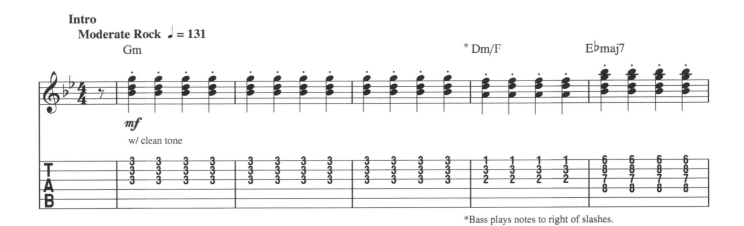

*Bass plays notes to right of slashes.

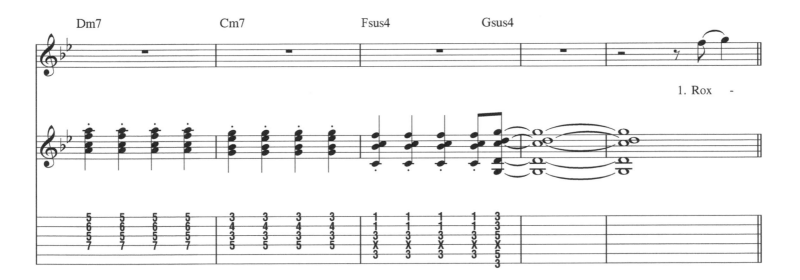

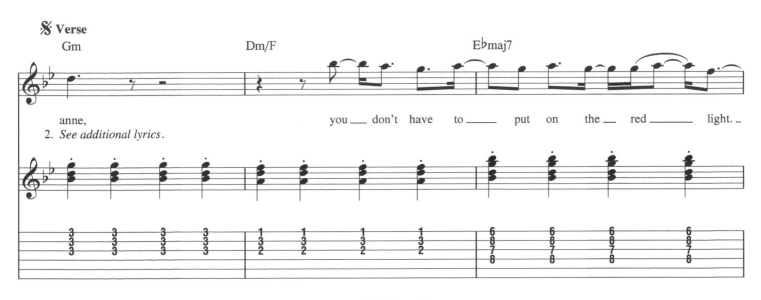

© 1978 G.M. SUMNER
Administered by EMI MUSIC PUBLISHING LIMITED
All Rights Reserved   International Copyright Secured   Used by Permission

Put on the red ___ light.

Put on the red ___ light.

Put on the red ___ light.

Oh.

Interlude

D.S. al Coda

2. I

mf

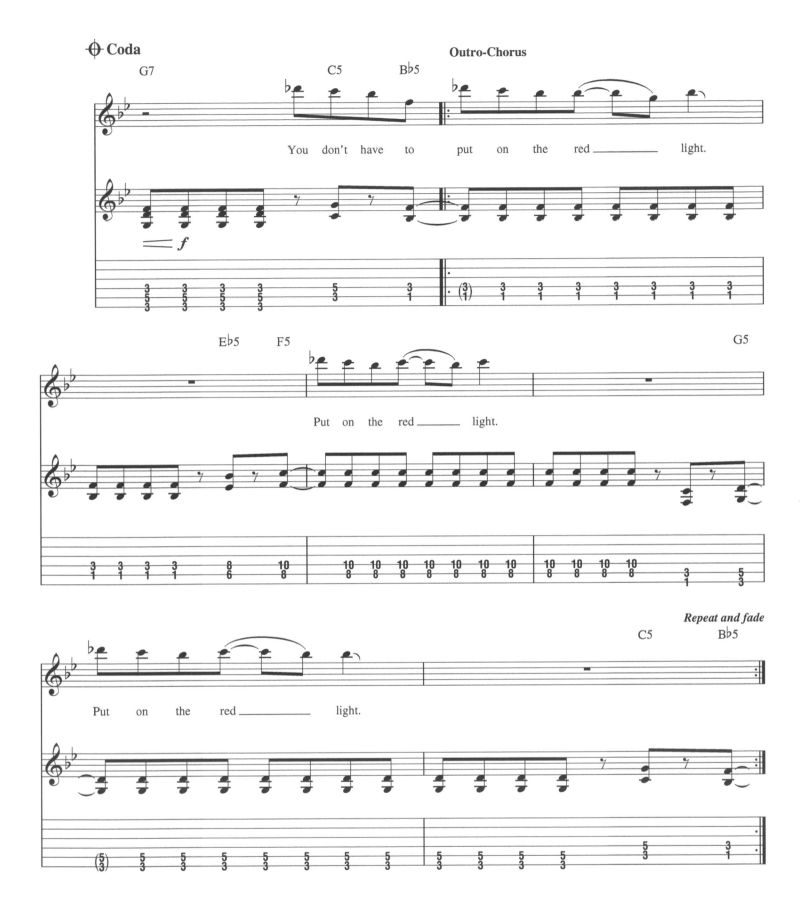

Additional Lyrics

2. I loved you since I knew ya,
    I wouldn't talk down to ya.
    I have to tell you just how I feel,
    I won't share you with another boy.
    I know my mind is made up,
    So put away your makeup.
    Told you once, I won't tell you again.
    It's a bad way.

Spirits in the Material World

Music and Lyrics by Sting

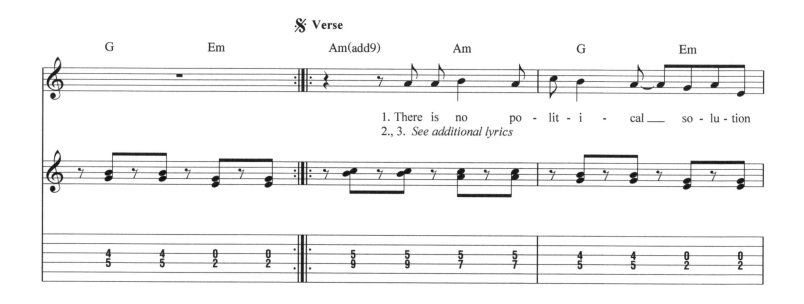

1. There is no po-lit-i-cal___ so-lu-tion
2., 3. *See additional lyrics*

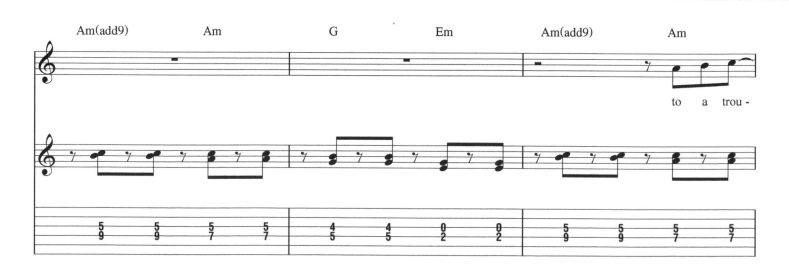

to a trou-

© 1981 G.M. SUMNER
Administered by EMI MUSIC PUBLISHING LIMITED
All Rights Reserved   International Copyright Secured   Used by Permission

Interlude

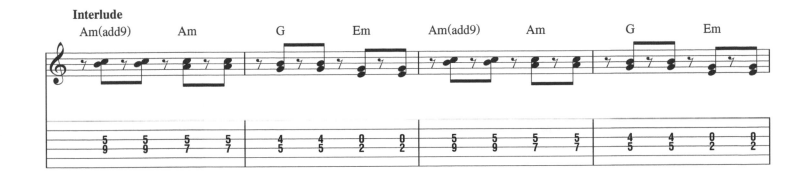

D.S. al Coda

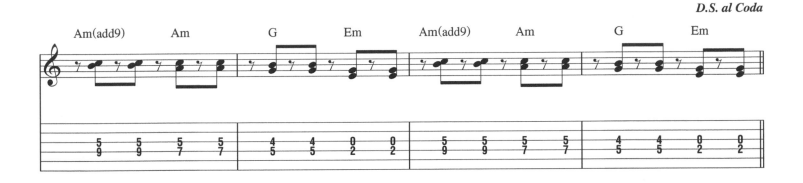

Coda

Outro

Repeat and fade

Are spir - its in the ma - te - rial world.

Additional Lyrics

2. Our so called leaders speak,
   With words they try to jail you.
   They subjugate the meek,
   But it's the rhetoric of failure.

3. Where does the answer lie?
   Living from day to day.
   If it's something we can't buy,
   There must be another way.

Synchronicity II
Music and Lyrics by Sting

© 1983 G.M. SUMNER
Administered by EMI MUSIC PUBLISHING LIMITED
All Rights Reserved   International Copyright Secured   Used by Permission

Bridge

Moth-er chants _ her lit - an - y _ of bore-dom and _ frus - tra - tion, but we know all _ her su - i - cides _ are _ fake.

Pre-Chorus

Dad - dy on - ly stares _ in - to _ the dis - tance.

P.M.

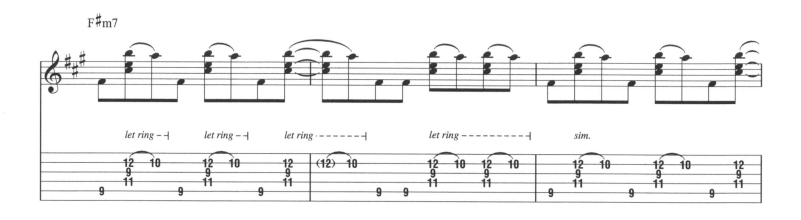

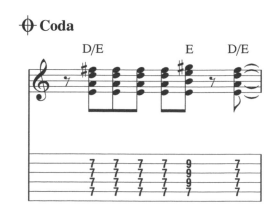

Chorus

Outro

Repeat and fade

Additional Lyrics

2. Another industrial ugly morning.
   The factory belches filth into the sky.
   He walks unhindered through the picket lines today.
   He doesn't think to wonder why.

Bridge 2. The secretaries pout and preen
   Like cheap tarts in a red-light street,
   But all he ever thinks to do is watch.

Pre-Chorus 2. And every single meeting with his so-called superior
   Is a humiliating kick in the crotch.

Chorus 2. Many miles away, something crawls to the surface
   Of a dark Scottish loch.

3. Another working day has ended.
   Only the rush hour hell to face.
   Packed like lemmings into shiny metal boxes.
   Contestants in a suicidal race.

Bridge 3. Daddy grips the wheel and stares
   Alone into the distance.
   He knows that something somewhere has to break.

Pre-Chorus 3. He sees the family home now, looming in his headlights.
   The pain upstairs that makes his eyeballs ache.

Walking on the Moon

Music and Lyrics by Sting

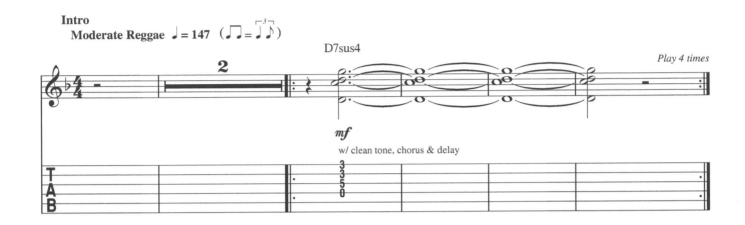

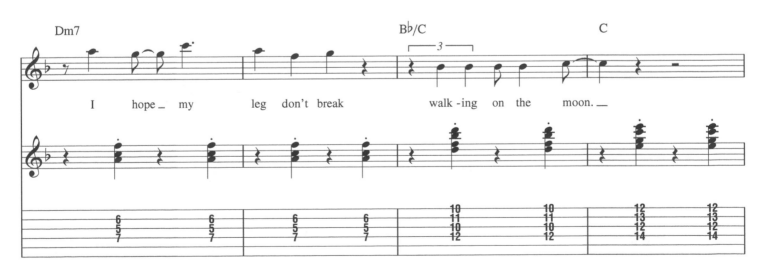

1. Gi - ant steps _ are what you take walk-ing on the moon. _

I hope _ my leg don't break walk-ing on the moon. _

© 1979 G.M. SUMNER
Administered by EMI MUSIC PUBLISHING LIMITED
All Rights Reserved International Copyright Secured Used by Permission

We could walk _ for - ev - er walk-ing on the moon. _

We could live _ to - geth - er walk-ing on, _ walk-ing on the moon. _

Interlude

w/ delay

*Sung 1st time only.

Verse

2. Walk - ing back _ from your house, walk - ing on the moon. _
3. *See additional lyrics*

delay off

Chorus

Some may say I'm wish-ing my days a - way;

no way. And, if it's a price I pay,

some say, "To - mor-row's an - oth - er day;

you'll stay." I may as well play.

Interlude

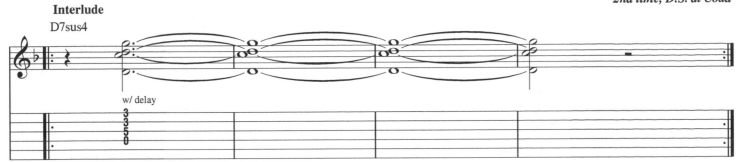

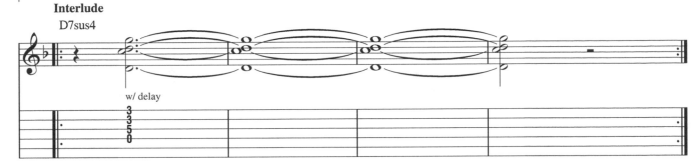

Outro

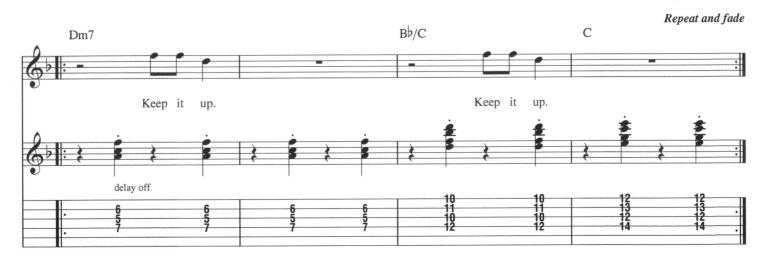

Additional Lyrics

3. Giant steps are what you take
   Walking on the moon.
   I hope my leg don't break
   Walking on the moon.
   We could walk forever
   Walking on the moon.
   We could live together
   Walking on, walking on the moon.

HAL•LEONARD GUITAR PLAY-ALONG

Complete song lists available online.

This series will help you play your favorite songs quickly and easily. Just follow the tab and listen to the audio to the hear how the guitar should sound, and then play along using the separate backing tracks. Audio files also include software to slow down the tempo without changing pitch. The melody and lyrics are included in the book so that you can sing or simply follow along.

INCLUDES TAB

VOL. 1 – ROCK .... 00699570 / $17.99
VOL. 2 – ACOUSTIC .... 00699569 / $16.99
VOL. 3 – HARD ROCK .... 00699573 / $17.99
VOL. 4 – POP/ROCK .... 00699571 / $16.99
VOL. 5 – THREE CHORD SONGS .... 00300985 / $16.99
VOL. 6 – '90S ROCK .... 00298615 / $16.99
VOL. 7 – BLUES .... 00699575 / $19.99
VOL. 8 – ROCK .... 00699585 / $16.99
VOL. 9 – EASY ACOUSTIC SONGS .... 00151708 / $16.99
VOL. 10 – ACOUSTIC .... 00699586 / $16.95
VOL. 11 – EARLY ROCK .... 00699579 / $15.99
VOL. 12 – ROCK POP .... 00291724 / $17.99
VOL. 14 – BLUES ROCK .... 00699582 / $16.99
VOL. 15 – R&B .... 00699583 / $17.99
VOL. 16 – JAZZ .... 00699584 / $16.99
VOL. 17 – COUNTRY .... 00699588 / $17.99
VOL. 18 – ACOUSTIC ROCK .... 00699577 / $15.95
VOL. 20 – ROCKABILLY .... 00699580 / $17.99
VOL. 21 – SANTANA .... 00174525 / $17.99
VOL. 22 – CHRISTMAS .... 00699600 / $15.99
VOL. 23 – SURF .... 00699635 / $17.99
VOL. 24 – ERIC CLAPTON .... 00699649 / $19.99
VOL. 25 – THE BEATLES .... 00198265 / $19.99
VOL. 26 – ELVIS PRESLEY .... 00699643 / $16.99
VOL. 27 – DAVID LEE ROTH .... 00699645 / $16.95
VOL. 28 – GREG KOCH .... 00699646 / $19.99
VOL. 29 – BOB SEGER .... 00699647 / $16.99
VOL. 30 – KISS .... 00699644 / $17.99
VOL. 32 – THE OFFSPRING .... 00699653 / $14.95
VOL. 33 – ACOUSTIC CLASSICS .... 00699656 / $19.99
VOL. 35 – HAIR METAL .... 00699660 / $17.99
VOL. 36 – SOUTHERN ROCK .... 00699661 / $19.99
VOL. 37 – ACOUSTIC UNPLUGGED .... 00699662 / $22.99
VOL. 38 – BLUES .... 00699663 / $17.99
VOL. 39 – '80s METAL .... 00699664 / $17.99
VOL. 40 – INCUBUS .... 00699668 / $17.95
VOL. 41 – ERIC CLAPTON .... 00699669 / $17.99
VOL. 42 – COVER BAND HITS .... 00211597 / $16.99
VOL. 43 – LYNYRD SKYNYRD .... 00699681 / $22.99
VOL. 44 – JAZZ GREATS .... 00699689 / $19.99
VOL. 45 – TV THEMES .... 00699718 / $14.95
VOL. 46 – MAINSTREAM ROCK .... 00699722 / $16.95
VOL. 47 – JIMI HENDRIX SMASH HITS .... 00699723 / $22.99
VOL. 48 – AEROSMITH CLASSICS .... 00699724 / $19.99
VOL. 49 – STEVIE RAY VAUGHAN .... 00699725 / $17.99
VOL. 50 – VAN HALEN: 1978-1984 .... 00110269 / $19.99
VOL. 51 – ALTERNATIVE '90s .... 00699727 / $14.99
VOL. 52 – FUNK .... 00699728 / $15.99
VOL. 53 – DISCO .... 00699729 / $14.99
VOL. 54 – HEAVY METAL .... 00699730 / $17.99
VOL. 55 – POP METAL .... 00699731 / $14.95
VOL. 57 – GUNS 'N' ROSES .... 00159922 / $19.99
VOL. 58 – BLINK 182 .... 00699772 / $17.99
VOL. 59 – CHET ATKINS .... 00702347 / $17.99
VOL. 60 – 3 DOORS DOWN .... 00699774 / $14.99
VOL. 62 – CHRISTMAS CAROLS .... 00699798 / $12.95
VOL. 63 – CREEDENCE CLEARWATER
        REVIVAL .... 00699802 / $17.99
VOL. 64 – ULTIMATE OZZY OSBOURNE .... 00699803 / $19.99
VOL. 66 – THE ROLLING STONES .... 00699807 / $19.99
VOL. 67 – BLACK SABBATH .... 00699808 / $17.99
VOL. 68 – PINK FLOYD –
        DARK SIDE OF THE MOON .... 00699809 / $17.99
VOL. 71 – CHRISTIAN ROCK .... 00699824 / $14.95

VOL. 74 – SIMPLE STRUMMING SONGS .. 00151706 / $19.99
VOL. 75 – TOM PETTY .... 00699882 / $19.99
VOL. 76 – COUNTRY HITS .... 00699884 / $16.99
VOL. 77 – BLUEGRASS .... 00699910 / $17.99
VOL. 78 – NIRVANA .... 00700132 / $17.99
VOL. 79 – NEIL YOUNG .... 00700133 / $24.99
VOL. 81 – ROCK ANTHOLOGY .... 00700176 / $22.99
VOL. 82 – EASY ROCK SONGS .... 00700177 / $17.99
VOL. 83 – SUBLIME .... 00369114 / $17.99
VOL. 84 – STEELY DAN .... 00700200 / $19.99
VOL. 85 – THE POLICE .... 00700269 / $17.99
VOL. 86 – BOSTON .... 00700465 / $19.99
VOL. 87 – ACOUSTIC WOMEN .... 00700763 / $14.99
VOL. 88 – GRUNGE .... 00700467 / $16.99
VOL. 89 – REGGAE .... 00700468 / $15.99
VOL. 90 – CLASSICAL POP .... 00700469 / $14.99
VOL. 91 – BLUES INSTRUMENTALS .... 00700505 / $19.99
VOL. 92 – EARLY ROCK
        INSTRUMENTALS .... 00700506 / $17.99
VOL. 93 – ROCK INSTRUMENTALS .... 00700507 / $17.99
VOL. 94 – SLOW BLUES .... 00700508 / $16.99
VOL. 95 – BLUES CLASSICS .... 00700509 / $15.99
VOL. 96 – BEST COUNTRY HITS .... 00211615 / $16.99
VOL. 97 – CHRISTMAS CLASSICS .... 00236542 / $14.99
VOL. 99 – ZZ TOP .... 00700762 / $17.99
VOL. 100 – B.B. KING .... 00700466 / $16.99
VOL. 101 – SONGS FOR BEGINNERS .... 00701917 / $14.99
VOL. 102 – CLASSIC PUNK .... 00700769 / $14.99
VOL. 104 – DUANE ALLMAN .... 00700846 / $22.99
VOL. 105 – LATIN .... 00700939 / $16.99
VOL. 106 – WEEZER .... 00700958 / $17.99
VOL. 107 – CREAM .... 00701069 / $17.99
VOL. 108 – THE WHO .... 00701053 / $17.99
VOL. 109 – STEVE MILLER .... 00701054 / $19.99
VOL. 110 – SLIDE GUITAR HITS .... 00701055 / $17.99
VOL. 111 – JOHN MELLENCAMP .... 00701056 / $14.99
VOL. 112 – QUEEN .... 00701052 / $16.99
VOL. 113 – JIM CROCE .... 00701058 / $19.99
VOL. 114 – BON JOVI .... 00701060 / $17.99
VOL. 115 – JOHNNY CASH .... 00701070 / $17.99
VOL. 116 – THE VENTURES .... 00701124 / $17.99
VOL. 117 – BRAD PAISLEY .... 00701224 / $16.99
VOL. 118 – ERIC JOHNSON .... 00701353 / $19.99
VOL. 119 – AC/DC CLASSICS .... 00701356 / $19.99
VOL. 120 – PROGRESSIVE ROCK .... 00701457 / $14.99
VOL. 121 – U2 .... 00701508 / $17.99
VOL. 122 – CROSBY, STILLS & NASH .... 00701610 / $16.99
VOL. 123 – LENNON & McCARTNEY
        ACOUSTIC .... 00701614 / $16.99
VOL. 124 – SMOOTH JAZZ .... 00200664 / $17.99
VOL. 125 – JEFF BECK .... 00701687 / $19.99
VOL. 126 – BOB MARLEY .... 00701701 / $17.99
VOL. 127 – 1970s ROCK .... 00701739 / $17.99
VOL. 129 – MEGADETH .... 00701741 / $17.99
VOL. 130 – IRON MAIDEN .... 00701742 / $17.99
VOL. 131 – 1990s ROCK .... 00701743 / $14.99
VOL. 132 – COUNTRY ROCK .... 00701757 / $15.99
VOL. 133 – TAYLOR SWIFT .... 00701894 / $16.99
VOL. 135 – MINOR BLUES .... 00151350 / $17.99
VOL. 136 – GUITAR THEMES .... 00701922 / $14.99
VOL. 137 – IRISH TUNES .... 00701966 / $17.99
VOL. 138 – BLUEGRASS CLASSICS .... 00701967 / $17.99

VOL. 139 – GARY MOORE .... 00702370 / $17.99
VOL. 140 – MORE STEVIE RAY VAUGHAN . 00702396 / $24.99
VOL. 141 – ACOUSTIC HITS .... 00702401 / $16.99
VOL. 142 – GEORGE HARRISON .... 00237697 / $17.99
VOL. 143 – SLASH .... 00702425 / $19.99
VOL. 144 – DJANGO REINHARDT .... 00702531 / $17.99
VOL. 145 – DEF LEPPARD .... 00702532 / $19.99
VOL. 146 – ROBERT JOHNSON .... 00702533 / $16.99
VOL. 147 – SIMON & GARFUNKEL .... 14041591 / $19.99
VOL. 148 – BOB DYLAN .... 14041592 / $17.99
VOL. 149 – AC/DC HITS .... 14041593 / $19.99
VOL. 150 – ZAKK WYLDE .... 02501717 / $19.99
VOL. 151 – J.S. BACH .... 02501730 / $16.99
VOL. 152 – JOE BONAMASSA .... 02501751 / $24.99
VOL. 153 – RED HOT CHILI PEPPERS .... 00702990 / $22.99
VOL. 155 – ERIC CLAPTON UNPLUGGED . 00703085 / $17.99
VOL. 156 – SLAYER .... 00703770 / $19.99
VOL. 157 – FLEETWOOD MAC .... 00101382 / $17.99
VOL. 159 – WES MONTGOMERY .... 00102593 / $22.99
VOL. 160 – T-BONE WALKER .... 00102641 / $17.99
VOL. 161 – THE EAGLES ACOUSTIC .... 00102659 / $19.99
VOL. 162 – THE EAGLES HITS .... 00102667 / $19.99
VOL. 163 – PANTERA .... 00103036 / $19.99
VOL. 164 – VAN HALEN: 1986-1995 .... 00110270 / $19.99
VOL. 165 – GREEN DAY .... 00210343 / $17.99
VOL. 166 – MODERN BLUES .... 00700764 / $16.99
VOL. 167 – DREAM THEATER .... 00111938 / $24.99
VOL. 168 – KISS .... 00113421 / $17.99
VOL. 169 – TAYLOR SWIFT .... 00115982 / $16.99
VOL. 170 – THREE DAYS GRACE .... 00117337 / $16.99
VOL. 171 – JAMES BROWN .... 00117420 / $16.99
VOL. 172 – THE DOOBIE BROTHERS .... 00119670 / $17.99
VOL. 173 – TRANS-SIBERIAN
        ORCHESTRA .... 00119907 / $19.99
VOL. 174 – SCORPIONS .... 00122119 / $19.99
VOL. 175 – MICHAEL SCHENKER .... 00122127 / $19.99
VOL. 176 – BLUES BREAKERS WITH JOHN
        MAYALL & ERIC CLAPTON .... 00122132 / $19.99
VOL. 177 – ALBERT KING .... 00123271 / $17.99
VOL. 178 – JASON MRAZ .... 00124165 / $17.99
VOL. 179 – RAMONES .... 00127073 / $17.99
VOL. 180 – BRUNO MARS .... 00129706 / $16.99
VOL. 181 – JACK JOHNSON .... 00129854 / $16.99
VOL. 182 – SOUNDGARDEN .... 00138161 / $17.99
VOL. 183 – BUDDY GUY .... 00138240 / $17.99
VOL. 184 – KENNY WAYNE SHEPHERD .. 00138258 / $17.99
VOL. 185 – JOE SATRIANI .... 00139457 / $19.99
VOL. 186 – GRATEFUL DEAD .... 00139459 / $17.99
VOL. 187 – JOHN DENVER .... 00140839 / $19.99
VOL. 188 – MÖTLEY CRÜE .... 00141145 / $19.99
VOL. 189 – JOHN MAYER .... 00144350 / $19.99
VOL. 190 – DEEP PURPLE .... 00146152 / $19.99
VOL. 191 – PINK FLOYD CLASSICS .... 00146164 / $17.99
VOL. 192 – JUDAS PRIEST .... 00151352 / $19.99
VOL. 193 – STEVE VAI .... 00156028 / $19.99
VOL. 194 – PEARL JAM .... 00157925 / $17.99
VOL. 195 – METALLICA: 1983-1988 .... 00234291 / $22.99
VOL. 196 – METALLICA: 1991-2016 .... 00234292 / $19.99

Prices, contents, and availability subject to change without notice.

HAL•LEONARD®
www.halleonard.com

0822